S0-BOI-958

LARRY FITZGERALD

Pro Bowl Receiver

By Brady Reinagel

Gareth Stevens
Publishing

Please visit our Web site www.garethstevens.com. For a free color catalog of all our high-quality books, call toll free 1-800-542-2595 or fax 1-877-542-2596.

Library of Congress Cataloging-in-Publication Data

Reinagel, Brady.
  Larry Fitzgerald: pro bowl receiver / Brady Reinagel.
      p. cm. — (Inspiring lives.)
  Includes index.
  ISBN 978-1-4339-3644-9 (pbk.)
  ISBN 978-1-4339-3645-6 (6-pack)
  ISBN 978-1-4339-3643-2 (library binding)
  1. Fitzgerald, Larry, 1983. 2. Football players—United States—Biography. I. Title.
  GV939.F55R45 2010
  796.332092—dc22
  [B]

                        2009037577

Published in 2010 by Gareth Stevens Publishing
111 East 14th Street, Suite 349
New York, NY 10003

Copyright © 2010 Gareth Stevens Publishing

Designer: Michael J. Flynn
Editor: Greg Roza

Photo credits: Cover (Larry Fitzgerald), pp. 1 (Larry Fitzgerald), 5 © Christian Petersen/ Getty Images; cover (field), p. 1 (field) Shutterstock.com; p. 7 © Ezra Shaw/Getty Images; p. 9 © Bob Rosato/Sports Illustrated/Getty Images; p. 11 © Paul Jasienski/Getty Images; p. 13 © Michael J. LeBrecht II/Sports Illustrated/Getty Images; p. 15 © Brian Bahr/ Getty Images; p. 17 © Craig Jones/Getty Images; p. 19 © Harry How/Getty Images; p. 21 © Dilip Vishwanat/Getty Images; pp. 23, 29 © Gene Lower/Getty Images; p. 25 © Doug Benc/Getty Images; p. 27 © Paul Spinelli/Getty Images.

Printed in the United States of America

CPSIA compliance information: Batch #CW10GS: For further information contact Gareth Stevens, New York, New York at 1-800-542-2595.

Contents

Hi, Larry!

Larry Fitzgerald is a pro football player.

He plays for the Arizona Cardinals.

Growing Up

Larry was born in 1983. He grew up in Minneapolis, Minnesota.

Larry's father is a sports writer. He also has shows on radio and TV. His name is Larry, too.

Ball Boy

Larry was a ball boy for the Minnesota Vikings when he was a teenager. The Vikings are a pro football team.

Playing for the Panthers

Larry played college football. He was a wide receiver for the Pittsburgh Panthers.

Larry played twenty-six games for the Panthers. He scored thirty-four touchdowns for his team!

Larry worked very hard to be a good football player. He was voted the best player in college football in 2003.

Going Pro

Larry joined the NFL in 2004. He scored eight touchdowns in his first year with the Arizona Cardinals.

Larry scored ten touchdowns in 2005.

He was one of the best wide receivers in

the NFL.

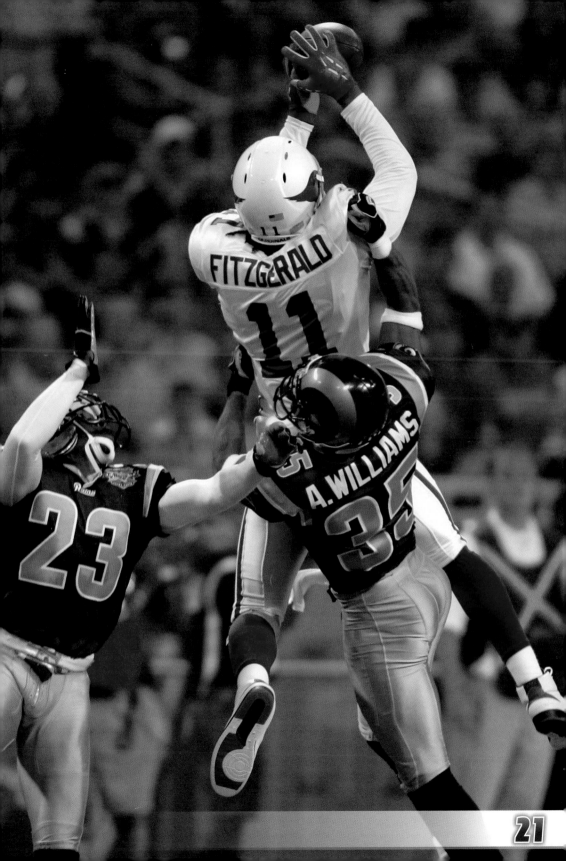

The Super Bowl!

Larry helped the Arizona Cardinals beat the Philadelphia Eagles in 2008. This meant the Cardinals were going to the Super Bowl!

Larry scored two touchdowns during the Super Bowl. He is very fast!

The Pro Bowl

The best football players are in a game called the Pro Bowl every year. Larry was named the best player of the 2008 Pro Bowl!

Giving Back

Larry helps raise money for charity. He also loves his fans!

Timeline

1983 Larry is born.

1998 Larry becomes a ball boy for the Minnesota Vikings.

2002 Larry plays on the Pittsburgh Panthers college football team.

2003 Larry is voted the best player in college football.

2004 Larry joins the Arizona Cardinals.

2008 Larry scores two touchdowns in the Super Bowl.

2008 Larry is named the best player in the Pro Bowl.

For More Information

Books:

Gilbert, Sara. *The Story of the Arizona Cardinals.* Mankato, MN: Creative Education, 2009.

Stewart, Mark. *Arizona Cardinals.* Chicago, IL: Norwood House Press, 2009.

Web Sites:

Arizona Cardinals: Larry Fitzgerald

www.azcardinals.com/team/roster/Larry-Fitzgerald/ 5e798db3-4421-453f-a489-c060d8eaf731

Larry Fitzgerald Official Web Site

www.larryfitzgerald11.com

NFL: Larry Fitzgerald

www.nfl.com/players/larryfitzgerald/profile?id=FIT437493

Glossary

charity: aid given to people in need

NFL: the pro football league in the United States. Short for National Football League

pro: someone who gets paid to play a sport

Super Bowl: the last football game of the year to decide the best team in the NFL

touchdown: a score of six points made by carrying or passing the football into the end zone

wide receiver: a fast football player who catches and runs with the ball to score points

Index